I0104874

Praise For *Positioned For Growth™*

"Does the world need another book on business growth? Well, it sure can use this one! Everyone talks about growth but Cory Mosley provides a clear blueprint for action! If you want to grow your business, read "Positioned for Growth" and be sure to ACT on the strategies."

- Bill Cates, CSP, CPAE
Author of *Radical Relevance*

"Cory and crew have completely changed our company's look, feel, and direction. His team exudes excellence and professionalism, which is the key to their success. I highly recommend embracing his Positioned For Growth framework and philosophy to grow your business."

- Timothy M. Brock, Founder & CEO
Permaseal Global LLC

"I have worked with Cory and his team for over a decade. His advice is always on point. My business would not be where it is today without him."

- Veronica Wyatt, Co-Founder
Pecan Jacks Ice Cream & Candy Kitchen

"Having Cory as an advisor in our twenty-year-old business has not only saved me a tremendous amount of money but has made me more than seven figures in additional revenue."

- Sean V. Bradley, Founder & President
Dealer Synergy

"Cory Mosley is a man on a mission, who has created a reputation for helping companies to have exponential growth. In his new book "Positioned For Growth" he shares the principles that have helped so many to grow their success. If you are serious about growing your success, then "Positioned For Growth" is a must read! This book will help you do more, be more and achieve more!"

- Dr. Willie Jolley, Hall of Fame Speaker, Sirius XM Radio Show Host and Best-Selling Author of *A Setback Is A Setup For A Comeback* & *An Attitude of Excellence!*

"Cory Mosley's *Positioned For Growth*™ is a must-read for any business leader committed to thriving in today's competitive market. Mosley's insights on fostering a sustainable growth mindset are particularly invaluable, making this guide not just relevant but essential for anyone looking to drive their business to new heights. Highly recommended!"

- Scott McKain, Author of *ICONIC* and *The Ultimate Customer Experience*

"Cory Mosley is bigger than life. He is an inspirational Speaker, thought leader, and business coach. But what really makes Cory unique is his approachability–He is down-to-earth, caring, and willing to go the extra mile to help others grow. I think the World of Cory and would recommend him to anyone looking for guidance."

- Michelle Denogean, Author and CMO Mind Trip, Inc.

"If there are two things Cory understands better than nearly everyone else, It's Business Growth & Branding, if you are looking to take your business to the next level, I highly recommend reaching out to him and his team."

- Steve Stauning, Best Selling Author of *Ridiculously Simple Customer Experience*

POSITIONED

A PROVEN STRATEGY TO MODERNIZE YOUR

FOR

BUSINESS AND ACHIEVE RECORD REVENUES

GROWTH

CORY MOSLEY, CSP

Positioned For Growth™

A proven strategy to modernize your business and achieve record revenues

Mosley Strategy Group LLC
2810 N. Parham Rd. Suite 360
Henrico, Va 23294

ISBN 9798218465711

First Edition
Cover design by Xiomara Mosley
Published by Mosley Strategy Group LLC

Bulk Ordering and quantity discounts are available to corporations, associations, and others. Contact xiomara@corymosley.com for details.

For more information, visit **corymosley.com**

Dedication

This book is dedicated to my wife, Xiomara, who has spent the last decade helping me get clients Positioned For Growth™ across multiple verticals and industries.

She is always ready to jump in and do whatever needs to be done without question or complaint.

And supporting me on my own positioning journey.

Table Of Contents

Foreword

Dr. Delatorro McNeal, II MS, CSP, CPAE

Congratulations! You've made a very smart decision to learn from Cory Mosley in this powerful, super-practical, tactical, and interactive results-based coaching program in this literary format. That's right. You're not just listening to, reading, and/or studying words on a page, but rather you're about to embark upon a masterclass of instructionally sound content that I know has been curated over decades of real-world experience.

Cory Mosley, CSP, has been a professional colleague and a personal friend for over 15 years. We met through the National Speakers Association, and from the time I first met Cory up until right this very moment, there are 4 qualities in Cory that are present in this amazing book that are timeless and worth their weight in gold.

First, Cory has always been committed to being a titan in his industry, and he's committed to helping you become a titan in your industry as well.

Second, Cory has always been extremely resourceful. Tony Robbins teaches the following, *"The problem is never resources, but always resourcefulness!"* This book provides you with so many wonderful and compelling resources for your overall success.

Third, Cory has always been very no-nonsense in his approach to success in business. He's always going to ask the hard questions that make you dig deep and get to the bottom-line source of whatever is not working in your business and life and fix the root so you can enjoy more of your revenue fruits. Likewise, in *Positioned For Growth*, you can expect Cory to pull no punches and dance around no bushes. His goal is simple and clear: to help modernize your business for maximum growth and achieve all-time record-breaking revenue.

Fourth, Cory is an absolutely vibrant

personality and an undercover comedian. As serious and intentional as Cory is about big business and making money, he's also a super kind, present, and naturally humorous business leader who can find a joke, antidote, and/or comical story that will make you laugh and smile from your heart.

I am certain that as you glean in this book from the blueprints, strategies, stories, and expert guidance that Cory will provide–you will also enjoy several refreshing moments of exuberant laughter.

In conclusion, no matter the business you have or the industry you are in, in order to scale, you must be Positioned for Growth.

I am certain, with mathematical exactitude, that you will LOVE your journey with Cory in this amazing book, and you will enjoy years of sustainable business growth and record-breaking revenues as a direct result of what you learn from the decades of wisdom and results that Cory Mosley has produced.

Cory Mosley

EXECUTE and ENJOY!

Dr. Delatorro L. McNeal, II MS, CSP, CPAE Hall of Fame Keynote Speaker and *WSJ* and *USA Today* Bestselling Author of *Shift Into a Higher Gear: Better Your Best and Live Life to the Fullest*

Introduction

I might not have seen it all, but I've seen a lot!

It is truly amazing to think that, as of writing this book, I have spent half of my life working with small business owners and C-suite executives inside major corporations and public companies.

At the age of 20 (although I doubt the client knew that at the time), I drafted an RFP response that saved his two-million-a-year I.T. contract with the then-named Bank Of New York. I was brought into the situation by a retired head of a mid-size CPA firm who dabbled in private CPA work from his co-working office in Short Hills, NJ, where I also had an office. He took a liking to me and knocked on my door one day and said, *"I don't know exactly what you do (neither did I at the time), but maybe you can help me."* It was the easiest (at least for me) three thousand dollars I had ever made for a few hours of work.

What a great exchange! He gave me three thousand dollars (which was a number I basically made up), and I helped his company keep two million dollars (gross revenue at least).

That experience, exchange, and moment twenty-four years ago set me on the path that brings us together today in the book. (R.I.P. Bob Friedman, the tough-as-nails man who knocked on my door, brought me that opportunity and shared the same affinity for green BMWs, although he had the 7-series and I drove a 3-series. Your mentorship made a difference.)

Since then, whether on location at a family-owned brick-and-mortar local business or on the 48th floor of a NASDAQ-listed company overlooking a major city skyline, my clients have always wanted the same thing: for their problems to be solved so their growth can continue or begin again.

I've worked with family businesses where siblings play tug-a-war over business decisions and can't be in the same room without a mediator (true story); I've been in secret meetings in restaurants where we've been partitioned off so as not to be spotted by an employee or business partner. I've been in crisis situations like the time I was running a major program for Volkswagen smack dab in the middle of the Diesel Gate scandal, and I've come into situations where the so-called "smartest person in the room" created business messes beyond measure.

As the famous saying goes, "Sometimes you can't see the picture when you are in the frame." This, in many ways, is the essence of consulting.

It has never been about being smarter than the client because I've worked with some really shrewd and intelligent individuals, but simply having the ability to look at a problem, challenge, or situation with a different perspective. As I process a client challenge or ask questions, I feel like Freddie Highmore's character Dr. Shaun Murphy in the TV series *The Good Doctor*, where you see these motion graphics pop up on the screen showing him processing data to come up with a solution to the patient's medical situation. And voila, a plan materializes to fix everything. Of course, we know it is never that simple. Or is it? Or at least can it be?

The one thing I know for sure is that no business owner or corporate CEO wants a stalled, stuck, or stagnant business. We all want to thrive and do it no matter the state of the economy or based on what political party is in power. I learned from the Godfather of Sales, Jefferey Gitomer, that it should never be *the economy* but *YOUR economy* that should matter most.

In the following pages, I share the strategies, tactics, and action plans honed over my twenty years of consulting so you can implement an evergreen approach to growing your business. This means the concepts will be applicable today and in the future to keep your business in growth mode.

The promise is to equip you with a reliable thought process and plan that won't shield you from problems or challenges but will keep you positioned for growth.

Part One: The Case For Positioning

BUSINESS

1

How a business becomes stuck, stalled, or stagnant

Success is a menace; it convinces smart people that they can't lose.
- Bill Gates

It's unfortunate to say, but I have been around the block enough times to see businesses that once seemed untouchable become Walgreens locations. I don't mean that in the *"strategically sold their business and made a pile of money kind of way."*

In many ways, through my interactions with business owners, I even predicated a few business implosions, albeit they took a few years to disappear fully. I think about the car dealership whose owner wanted to show loyalty to his sales manager, and upon his becoming ill, let him manage the sales team and work deals from home. I couldn't have been the only one who could've predicted the irreparable damage that decision would do to the sales at the dealership. They never recovered.

I think about the local organic-themed eatery that opened near my house that my wife and I visited with a kid-like excitement as part of our attempt to eat healthier, only to be overwhelmed by their complicated order process involving paper, pencil, and a hundred customizable options. Yes, the food was fresh and organic, but the customer experience was confusing and felt like too much work, which meant the juice would not be worth the squeeze for us. For the record, I'm always okay with being wrong about something, but I knew that if they didn't change their processes, they wouldn't make it, and sadly they didn't.

The truth is unless something dramatic happens, most business erosion is death by a thousand cuts or the frog who meets his maker in the water that slowly heats up to boil until it's too late for the frog to leap out. This is what happens to businesses.

When we think about becoming stuck, stalled, or stagnant, we are saying that growth has stopped. While you may have an opinion as to why, the true reasons are often matter-of-fact, while the owner or CEO's opinions might be more emotional or further away from the truth.

Here are some real reasons why businesses become stuck, stalled, and stagnant:

1. **Market Saturation:** The market may be fully saturated with competitors, making it difficult to attract new customers or increase market share.

2. **Lack of Innovation:** Failure to innovate or adapt to changing market trends and customer preferences can lead to stagnation.

3. Poor Marketing Strategies: Ineffective marketing and branding efforts can result in low visibility and reduced customer acquisition.

4. Operational Inefficiencies: Inefficient processes, outdated technology, or poor management can hinder productivity and growth.

5. Financial Constraints: Limited access to capital or poor financial management can restrict the ability to invest in growth opportunities.

6. Leadership Issues: Inadequate leadership, lack of vision, or internal conflicts among the management team can negatively impact growth.

7. Customer Retention Problems: High customer churn rates or dissatisfaction can prevent a business from growing its customer base.

8. Regulatory and Compliance Issues: Navigating complex regulatory environments or facing legal challenges can be costly and time-consuming, affecting growth.

9. **Economic Conditions:** Broader economic factors such as recessions, inflation, or changes in consumer spending habits can impact business growth.

10. **Talent Shortages:** Difficulty in attracting and retaining skilled employees can limit a company's ability to scale.

11. **Supply Chain Disruptions:** Issues with suppliers or logistics can lead to delays and increased costs, affecting growth.

12. **Competitive Pressure:** Intense competition can erode market share and profitability, making it hard to grow.

13. **Customer Misalignment:** Not fully understanding or meeting customer needs can lead to a disconnect and reduced sales.

14. Scalability Issues: The business model or infrastructure may not be scalable, limiting the ability to handle increased demand.

15. Poor Strategic Planning: Lack of clear, long-term strategic planning can result in missed opportunities and stagnant growth.

16. Technological Lag: Failing to adopt new technologies or digital transformation can make a business less competitive.

17. Brand Perception: Negative brand perception or reputation issues can deter potential customers and partners.

I am not a big fan of *excuses*, but I believe in *reasons*, such as *the dog ate my homework* being an excuse, but *the dog ate my homework because I fed it to him* being a reason—albeit a stupid one.

As you review the list, how many of those in the list qualify as reasons, and how many are excuses for you potentially in your business?

When a business owner or executive says to me, *"Cory, I'm not really sure how this happened,"* I'm pretty sure we can go back through the list and figure it out quickly because the statement *"We didn't see this coming"* is rarely an accurate one.

Chapter Summary

This chapter explains how businesses can become stuck, stalled, or stagnant due to gradual issues such as market saturation, lack of innovation, poor marketing, operational inefficiencies, and leadership problems. It is important to identify these root causes to prevent business decline.

Action Items

1. **Assess Market Position:** Evaluate market saturation and explore niche opportunities.
2. **Encourage Innovation:** Stay updated with market trends and foster a culture of innovation.

3. **Improve Marketing:** Enhance visibility through effective digital marketing and social media strategies.
4. **Optimize Operations:** Conduct an operational audit and streamline processes for better efficiency.
5. **Strengthen Financial Management:** Review financial practices and develop a robust financial plan.
6. **Enhance Leadership:** Invest in leadership development and ensure clear communication within the team.
7. **Focus on Customer Needs:** Gather feedback regularly and adapt offerings to meet customer demands.

CHANGE
TRYING TO STEP FOWARD OUT...
CHANGE

2

Change is easy (you go first)

The secret of change is to focus all of your energy not on fighting the old but on building the new.
- Socrates

Let's have a heart-to-heart about something we all face but rarely talk about: change. If you've ever felt like making changes in your business is an uphill battle, you're not alone. I've been in your shoes and helped many others who've been right where you are now. Let's dive into why making changes can be tough and why trying to do it all overnight can set you up for failure, even if you have the best intentions.

Why We Resist Change

First, let's get real about why change is hard. As humans, we naturally resist change because we crave stability and predictability. In business, this resistance can be even more intense for a few reasons:

1. **Fear of the Unknown:** Change brings uncertainty, which can be scary. You might worry about how it will impact your finances, team, or customers.

2. **Comfort with the Status Quo:** It becomes second nature when you've been doing things a certain way for a while. Changing it up feels like stepping into the unknown, and that comfort zone can be tough to leave behind.

3. **Threats to Competence:** Change often means learning new skills or adopting new ways of thinking. Feeling anxious about whether you can rise to the challenge is natural.

4. **Past Failures:** If you've tried to make changes before and it didn't go well, it's easy to become skeptical and cautious about trying again.

Let's Be Like The Ritz-Carlton

My phone started ringing one afternoon, and after answering, I was greeted by my client's plea, *"Cory, I'm having a problem with one of my senior managers."* Ok, I said and then proceeded to have him explain to me the problem; *"Well, I want everybody here to treat our customers like they are guests at the Ritz-Carlton; if a customer asks where the bathroom is, I don't want them just to point I want my employees to escort the customer all the way to the rest room. But it doesn't seem like my managers are getting it."* I've always found that one of the benefits of working with a client for several years and understanding many, if not all, of the dynamics of their business and personality is the ability to predict their behavior in a given situation. This call was no exception. I asked if he had basically called a meeting with his management team, stood up and announced to everyone that they would now be treating every customer like a guess at the Ritz-Carlton, gave his bathroom example, and then sat back down moving on to the next item on the meeting's agenda. He paused momentarily to process my question and said, *"Well, not exactly, but something like that."* I then asked him a series of questions for his consideration, including, *"Do you know if your manager has ever stayed at a Ritz-Carlton or if he even believes that a hotel room is worth six, seven, or a thousand dollars a night?"* His response was, *"I didn't even think about it that way, thanks, Mosley"* (what most clients call me).

The Problem with Drastic Changes

Thinking that big, sweeping changes will quickly solve your problems is tempting. I get it. But here's why drastic overnight transformations often don't work:

1. **Lack of Preparation:** Big changes need careful planning. Rushing into them

without a solid plan can create chaos and confusion.

2. **Overwhelming Your Team:** Sudden changes can overwhelm and frustrate your employees. They need time to understand and adapt to new ways of working.
3. **Implementation Gaps:** Drastic changes can reveal gaps in skills and resources. Without proper support, your team might struggle to keep up.
4. **Cultural Misalignment:** If changes don't align with your company's culture, you will likely face significant pushback, making it hard to implement them successfully.

Avoiding Change for Change's Sake

Sometimes, we get caught up in the hype and chase the latest trends or make changes just to shake things up. But not all change is good change. Here's why:

1. **Misallocation of Resources:** Investing time and money into unnecessary changes diverts resources from areas truly needing attention.

2. **Disruption Without Value:** Changes that don't add real value can disrupt your operations and create confusion, ultimately harming your business.

3. **Eroding Trust and Morale:** Frequent, purposeless changes can erode trust and morale among your team. They might start seeing change as arbitrary and lose faith in your leadership.

Change is tough, but it's also essential for growth. Unlike my client's approach of simply announcing change and trying to force it via command, you will have the opportunity to approach change more strategically, producing significantly better growth results in the following chapters.

With our Positioned For Growth™ approach, you can successfully implement changes that benefit your business. I have seen this happen repeatedly, and I know you can do it, too.

Chapter Summary

Change is challenging due to human nature's preference for stability and fear of the unknown. Drastic overnight changes often fail because they lack preparation, overwhelm teams, and misalign with company culture. Successful change requires strategic planning, gradual implementation, and alignment with business values and goals.

Action Items

1. **Identify and Address Fears:** Understand and address the specific fears and uncertainties that your team may have about upcoming changes.
2. **Plan Thoroughly:** Develop a detailed plan for implementing changes, including timelines, resources needed, and potential challenges.
3. **Communicate Clearly:** Ensure clear and consistent communication about the changes,

including the reasons behind them and the benefits they will bring.

4. Involve the Team: Engage employees in the change process by seeking their input and involving them in planning and implementation.

5. Provide Support: Offer training and resources to help your team adapt to new skills and processes.

6. Monitor Progress: Regularly check in on the progress of the change implementation and make adjustments as needed.

7. Celebrate Successes: Recognize and celebrate small wins and milestones to maintain motivation and build confidence in the change process.

WHAT!
DO?
WHA??

3
You can't mandate productivity (Steve Jobs had it right)

> *You can't mandate productivity; it's an organization's responsibility to equip its team with the tools they need to be successful.*
> *- Steve Jobs*

As a business owner, you understand the importance of productivity. It is the engine that drives growth, fuels innovation, and propels your organization toward its goals. However, one common misconception is that productivity can simply be mandated from the top down. The reality is far more nuanced. Productivity cannot be enforced by mere edict;

it must be cultivated and nurtured. This chapter will explore why mandating productivity is ineffective and how providing your employees with the right tools and resources can lead to genuine, sustainable productivity.

The Illusion of Mandated Productivity

Command and Control: An Outdated Approach

In the early days of industrialization, the command-and-control management style was prevalent. This approach relied on strict oversight, rigid hierarchies, and an emphasis on compliance. Workers were seen as cogs in a machine, and productivity was measured by output volume alone. While this method may have worked in the past, it is increasingly ineffective in today's dynamic, knowledge-based economy.

The Human Element

Mandating productivity fails to account for the human element of work. Employees are not machines; they have needs, motivations, and aspirations. Productivity mandates often ignore these factors, leading to disengagement and burnout. Employees subjected to constant pressure without adequate support will likely experience stress and reduced job satisfaction, ultimately undermining productivity. Now I get it; as someone who would be considered Gen-X, and as someone from the auto industry, I came from the world of round-the-clock working, and the best sign that you were doing a great job is when your boss wasn't communicating with you. Spoiler alert: that's all changed!

The Limitations of Top-Down Directives

Top-down directives can create a culture of compliance rather than commitment. When employees are forced to follow orders without understanding the bigger picture or having a say in the process, they are less likely to be invested in the outcome. This lack of engagement can result in minimal effort, reduced innovation, and a reluctance to go above and beyond.

The Case for Empowerment

Understanding Employee Needs

Understanding what your employees need to succeed is essential to fostering productivity. This involves recognizing their individual strengths, addressing their challenges, and providing the necessary resources. Employees who feel supported and valued are more likely to be motivated and productive. In all fairness to your intelligence, my rationale for reaffirming this isn't because I believe it is new information but rather information that has potentially become a low priority for you as a leader to execute because of the daily focus on sales growth and profitability.

Equipping Employees with the Right Tools

Providing employees with the tools they need to succeed is a multifaceted approach encompassing physical resources, technology, training, and a conducive work environment.

Physical Resources and Technology

Ensure that your employees have access to up-to-date equipment and technology that enhances their efficiency. Outdated tools can significantly hinder, leading to frustration and wasted time. Investing in modern technology can streamline workflows and enable employees to focus on high-value tasks.

Training and Development

Continuous learning and development opportunities are crucial for maintaining a skilled and adaptable workforce. Offer training programs that help employees enhance their skills and stay abreast of industry trends. Encouraging professional growth not only boosts productivity but also fosters loyalty and retention. During my years running a consultancy focused exclusively on the auto industry, I was always saddened when someone I knew desperately needed to attend one of our workshops could not because the manager was unwilling to invest in getting them the education they desperately needed.

And just for clarity, we aren't talking about thousands of dollars; a workshop ticket back then was around three hundred and ninety-nine dollars, which was without a doubt a drop in the bucket compared to the number of revenue opportunities the potential attendee was responsible for.

To this day, I find it baffling that one person can stand in the way of getting so many people they lead help when the ROI, in most cases, is off the charts.

A Conducive Work Environment

The physical and psychological work environment plays a significant role in productivity. Create a workspace that is comfortable, organized, and conducive to focus. Additionally, it fosters a positive organizational culture that encourages collaboration, creativity, and open communication.

The Role of Leadership

Leading by Example

As a business owner or company leader, your actions set the tone for the organization. Demonstrate the values and behaviors you wish to see in your employees. Show commitment, integrity, and a strong work ethic. When employees see their leaders embodying these qualities, they are more likely to follow suit.

Empowering Through Trust

Trust is a cornerstone of effective leadership. Trust your employees to take ownership of their work and make decisions.

Micromanagement stifles creativity and autonomy, whereas trust empowers employees to take initiative and innovate.

Providing Clear Goals and Feedback

Set clear, achievable goals that align with the organization's vision. Ensure that employees understand how their contributions fit into the larger picture. Regular feedback is also essential. Constructive feedback helps employees improve, while recognition and praise reinforce positive behaviors and accomplishments.

During my years in sales management, I worked for a guy who thought very highly of himself, to say the least. I never forgot my time working with him for several reasons, but in this context, one of them was the fact that he rarely acknowledged the record-breaking work that my team was doing. I was running the e-commerce department for one of the largest Lexus dealerships in the country. I had built the largest e-commerce sales operation for that brand during that time, responsible for millions of dollars of net profit. These numbers were not being done at the time in the retail auto industry. Although it's been over twenty years, I still remember all the hard work I put into our monthly report, which had to be hand-calculated back then, showing our leads, appointment show ratios, conversions, gross profit, closing ratios, and high customer feedback scores. I remember it like it was yesterday, proudly walking to his desk, handing him this report, and watching him open his drawer, lift a bunch of other papers, and bury it under them. I was devastated and, as you can see, I never forgot it.

I looked at him differently after that day, which would contribute to a decline in the voracity of my work at that organization. Always remember small things matter, particularly when it comes to how your team views you as a leader.

Building a Culture of Accountability

Shared Responsibility

Fostering a culture of accountability means that everyone in the organization, from top to bottom, takes responsibility for their actions and contributions. This shared responsibility encourages employees to take ownership of their work and strive for excellence.

Encouraging Collaboration

Collaboration enhances productivity by leveraging the team's collective strengths and expertise. Encourage cross-functional collaboration and create opportunities for employees to work together on projects. Collaborative efforts often yield innovative solutions and drive higher performance.

Measuring Success

Defining Metrics

To gauge the effectiveness of your productivity initiatives, it is important to define clear metrics. These metrics should go beyond output volume and consider factors such as quality, efficiency, employee engagement, and customer satisfaction.

Continuous Improvement

Productivity is not a static goal but an ongoing journey. Regularly review and assess your strategies and make necessary adjustments. Encourage a mindset of continuous improvement within your organization, where employees are motivated to seek better ways of working.

Mandating productivity is an outdated and ineffective approach that overlooks the complexities of human motivation and engagement. Instead, focus on equipping your employees with the tools, resources, and support they need to succeed. By understanding their needs, fostering a positive work environment, and leading with trust and clarity, you can create a culture of empowerment and accountability. This approach enhances productivity and drives sustainable growth and success for your organization. Remember, productivity is not about enforcing compliance; it is about inspiring commitment and excellence.

Chapter Summary

Mandating productivity from the top down is ineffective because it ignores the human element and complexities of motivation. Instead, productivity should be cultivated by understanding employee needs, providing the right tools and resources, and fostering a positive work environment. Empowering employees through trust, clear goals, and feedback leads to genuine, sustainable productivity and organizational success.

Action Items

1. **Understand Employee Needs:** Regularly assess and address individual strengths, challenges, and resource requirements.
2. **Equip with Up-to-date Technology:** Invest in modern tools and equipment to enhance efficiency and reduce frustration.
3. **Offer Continuous Training:** Provide ongoing learning and development opportunities to keep skills current and employees motivated.
4. **Create a Conducive Work Environment:** Design a comfortable, organized workspace that fosters focus and creativity.
5. **Lead by Example:** Demonstrate commitment, integrity, and a strong work ethic to inspire employees.
6. **Empower Through Trust:** Delegate responsibilities and avoid micromanagement to encourage initiative and innovation.
7. **Set Clear Goals and Provide Feedback:** Ensure employees understand their role in the bigger picture and provide regular, constructive feedback.

PROPER
FOR GROWTH
PROPER
FOR
GROWTH

4
Why Positioning Trumps Change

Positioning is not what you do to a product; it is what you do to the prospect's mind.
- Al Ries

It's often tempting to believe that dramatic, overnight changes can solve deep-rooted problems and drive rapid success in the business world. However, the reality is that sustainable growth and long-term success are rarely achieved through quick fixes. Instead, positioning your business for growth is a more strategic and effective approach. This chapter explores why positioning for growth trumps attempting sudden, sweeping changes and how you can implement this mindset in your organization.

Understanding Positioning for Growth

Positioning for growth involves creating a solid foundation and strategic roadmap that guides your business toward its goals. It's about making deliberate, well-informed decisions that set the stage for sustainable progress. This approach focuses on enhancing your business's core strengths, optimizing processes, and aligning your team with a clear vision.

The Pitfalls of Overnight Changes

1. Lack of Stability

When businesses attempt drastic changes overnight, they often destabilize their operations. Employees may feel uncertain, workflows can become disjointed, and the quality of products or services may suffer. This instability can lead to a loss of customer trust and damage the business's reputation.

2. Short-Term Focus

Overnight changes are frequently driven by short-term goals. While these may provide immediate results, they often neglect long-term sustainability. A business that focuses solely on short-term gains may find itself in a cycle of constant upheaval, never truly establishing a solid foundation for future success.

3. Resistance to Change

Humans naturally resist change, especially when it is sudden and poorly communicated. Overnight changes can lead to confusion, fear, and resistance among employees. This resistance can impede the implementation of new strategies and negatively affect morale.

The Advantages of Positioning for Growth

1. Strategic Planning

Positioning for growth involves comprehensive strategic planning. This means setting clear, achievable goals and outlining the steps necessary to reach them. By taking the time to plan, businesses can anticipate challenges and devise strategies to overcome them, ensuring a smoother path to success.

2. Incremental Improvement

Rather than attempting to overhaul the entire business at once, positioning for growth focuses on incremental improvements. This allows businesses to make steady progress while minimizing disruption. Over time, these small changes compound, leading to significant growth and improvement.

3. Enhanced Employee Engagement

When employees are involved in a strategic growth plan, they are more likely to understand and support the changes.

Positioning for growth fosters a culture of continuous improvement and collaboration, leading to higher employee engagement and productivity.

4. Customer-Centric Approach
Positioning your business for growth requires deeply understanding your customers' needs and preferences. By prioritizing customer satisfaction and loyalty, businesses can create products and services that resonate with their target audience, driving long-term success.

Chapter Summary

This chapter emphasizes the ineffectiveness of rapid, dramatic changes to solve deep-rooted business issues and drive sustainable success. Instead, it advocates for positioning a business for growth through strategic planning, incremental improvements, and aligning team efforts. The chapter also highlights the pitfalls of overnight changes, such as instability, short-term focus, and resistance to change, and contrasts these with the benefits of a growth-oriented approach.

Action Items

1. **Develop a Comprehensive Strategic Plan:** Set clear, achievable goals and outline the steps necessary to reach them.
2. **Focus on Incremental Improvements:** Implement small, steady changes that minimize disruption and lead to significant growth over time.
3. **Engage Employees in the Growth Plan:** Involve employees in strategic planning to foster a culture of continuous improvement and collaboration.
4. **Prioritize Customer Understanding:** Conduct market research to deeply understand customer needs and preferences and tailor products and services accordingly.
5. **Communicate Changes Effectively:** Ensure clear communication about changes to reduce employee resistance and confusion.
6. **Monitor and Adjust Strategies:** Review progress regularly and be prepared to adjust

strategies based on feedback and changing circumstances.

7. **Strengthen Core Business Areas:** Enhance the core strengths of your business and optimize processes to support sustainable growth.

Cory Mosley

Part Two: The Positioned For Growth™ 5 Pillars

PROSITIONED
FOR GROWTH

5
Mindset (scarcity or abundance)

Optimism is the faith that leads to achievement. Nothing can be done without hope and confidence.
- Helen Keller

Let's have a heart-to-heart about something that's often overlooked but absolutely critical to your business success: your belief system and mindset.

The Foundation of Success: Belief System

First things first, let's talk about belief. Your belief system is the lens through which you view the world and, more importantly, your business. Do you see challenges as insurmountable obstacles or as opportunities for growth? Your perspective here can make or break your ability to seize new opportunities and take calculated risks.

Think about it. Every successful business starts with a belief. Whether you founded your business or are in an executive leadership role, you should strongly believe in your product, service, and, most importantly, yourself. When you have a solid belief in your capabilities and vision, navigating the tumultuous waters of entrepreneurship becomes much easier. You'll find that your belief system is like the rudder of a ship; it steers you toward your goals, even when the seas get rough.

The Mindset Shift: From Fixed to Growth

Now, let's shift gears and dive into mindset. Carol Dweck, a renowned psychologist, introduced the concept of fixed and growth mindsets. A fixed mindset is where you believe your abilities and intelligence are static. Conversely, a growth mindset means you see your abilities as something you can develop through hard work and dedication.

As a business owner, adopting a growth mindset is crucial. Why? Because the business landscape is ever-changing. What worked yesterday might not work tomorrow. If you're stuck in a fixed mindset, you'll resist change and miss out on opportunities for innovation and improvement.

Let's say your business hits a rough patch. A fixed mindset might make you think, *"I'm just not cut out for this."* But with a growth mindset, you'd approach it differently: *"What can I learn from this? How can I improve?"* This shift in thinking opens up a world of possibilities. It transforms failures into learning experiences and setbacks into stepping stones.

Seizing Opportunities and Taking Risks

Belief and mindset are the bedrock, but what about the action? To position your business for explosive growth, you need to be ready to seize opportunities and take risks. This doesn't mean being reckless. It means being calculated and informed in your decisions.

Think of it like this: opportunities are like buses. There's always another one coming, but you must be prepared to jump on. You'll miss that bus if you're not confident in your abilities (belief) or afraid to step out of your comfort zone (mindset). But if you've cultivated a strong belief in yourself and embraced a growth mindset, you'll be ready to take that leap, knowing that even if things don't go as planned, you have the resilience to bounce back and learn from the experience.

Chapter Summary

This chapter explored the profound impact of belief systems and mindsets on business success. By embracing a growth mindset and fostering a strong belief in your abilities, you position yourself to seize opportunities and take calculated risks, paving the way for explosive business growth.

Action Items

1. **Self-Reflection:** Take time to reflect on your current belief system. Are there any limiting beliefs holding you back? Write them down and challenge them.
2. **Growth Mindset:** Commit to adopting a growth mindset. Embrace challenges, persist through obstacles, and see effort as the path to mastery.
3. **Learn Continuously:** Make learning a habit. Read books, attend seminars, and seek out mentors. The more you know, the more confident you'll become in seizing opportunities.

4. **Set Clear Goals:** Define what success looks like for you and your business. Having a clear vision will strengthen your belief in your ability to achieve it.
5. **Take Calculated Risks:** Identify potential opportunities and evaluate the risks involved. Make informed decisions, and don't be afraid to step out of your comfort zone.
6. **Build a Support System:** Surround yourself with positive, like-minded individuals who encourage your growth and challenge you to be your best.
7. **Celebrate Wins:** Acknowledge and celebrate your successes, no matter how small. This reinforces your belief in your capabilities and motivates you to keep pushing forward.

SALE
LE OF THE CENTURY
SALE OF THE CENTUR
SALE OF THE CENTURY
SALE SALE
OF THE
SALE OF THE CENTURY
SALE OF THE CENTURY
SAL

6
Sales (strategy or market volatility)

Nothing happens until someone sells something.
- Arthur H. "Red" Motley

We can't talk about business growth without talking about sales. Now, let's be clear: having a sales strategy isn't just a nice-to-have–it's a must-have, especially in today's ever-changing market landscape. Market volatility can be a real challenge, but with the right sales strategy, you can weather the storm and come out stronger on the other side.

The Power of a Sales Strategy

Imagine trying to navigate a ship without a map or compass. You'd be adrift, constantly reacting to the waves and winds without a clear direction. A sales strategy is your map and compass in the business world. It provides direction, helps you allocate resources efficiently, and keeps your team aligned and focused on common goals.

But here's the kicker: having a sales strategy is not enough. You need a modern strategy that reflects the needs and behaviors of today's buyers. The old tactics that might have worked a decade ago are likely outdated. Today's buyers are more informed, more connected, and have higher expectations than ever before.

Why Modern Sales Strategies Matter

In the past, sales strategies often revolved around cold calling and direct mail campaigns. While these tactics might still have a place, they are far from sufficient. Modern buyers do their homework. They research online, read reviews, compare products, and expect personalized interactions. Your sales strategy must meet these expectations head-on.

A modern sales strategy leverages technology, data, and customer insights to create a personalized experience. It involves using customer relationship management (CRM) systems to track interactions, analyzing data to understand buying patterns, and employing digital marketing techniques to nurture leads. It's about being proactive rather than reactive, anticipating your customers' needs, and engaging with them on their terms.

Pitfalls of a Poor Sales Strategy

Let's discuss the pitfalls of having an outdated or poorly executed sales strategy. One major pitfall is inconsistency. Without a clear strategy, your sales efforts can be disjointed and unfocused, leading to missed opportunities and wasted resources. Another pitfall is failing to adapt. The market is constantly evolving, and if your strategy doesn't evolve, you'll quickly fall behind your competitors.

Moreover, an ineffective sales strategy can demotivate your team. When salespeople don't have a clear plan to follow, they can become frustrated and disengaged, affecting morale and your bottom line.

Time for a Change

Now is the time to challenge and modernize your current sales strategy. It's time to be open-minded, to question old assumptions, and to embrace new ways of thinking. Change can be daunting, but it's also an opportunity for growth and innovation. By modernizing your sales strategy, you're positioning your business to thrive, no matter what the market throws at you.

Chapter Summary

A modern, well-thought-out sales strategy is crucial in today's volatile market. It helps you stay ahead of the competition, meet buyers' evolving needs, and ensure your sales efforts are consistent and effective. Embrace change, leverage technology, and align your strategy with today's buyer expectations.

Action Items

1. **Assess Your Current Strategy:** Evaluate what's working and not in your current sales approach.
2. **Understand Your Buyer Persona:** Research and update your knowledge of your target customers' behaviors, needs, and preferences.
3. **Leverage Technology:** Invest in CRM systems and other sales tools that can provide valuable insights and streamline your processes.
4. **Train Your Team:** Ensure your sales team has the skills and knowledge to implement the new strategy.

5. **Personalize Your Approach:** Use data to create personalized interactions with your customers.
6. **Monitor and Adapt:** Regularly review your strategy's effectiveness and be prepared to make adjustments as needed.
7. **Engage in Continuous Learning:** Stay updated on the latest sales trends and technologies to keep your strategy current.

MARKETHG CAMPAIGN
MARKETING CAMPAIGN PICK?
WHICH CARKETING PICK?
WHICH MARKETING IDEAS
IDEAS
MARKETING CAMPAIGN
MARKETING IDEAS
MARKETING IDEAS
DOR?
MARKETING IDEAS
MARKETING CAMPAIGN
MARKETING CAMPAIGN IDEAS
MARKETING CAMPAIGN
WHICH MARKETING CAMPAIGN
MARKETING

7
Marketing (cute or clear)

The aim of marketing is to know and understand the customer so well the product or service fits him and sells itself.
- Peter Drucker

Now, I want to dive into modern marketing, a topic close to my heart and crucial for your business growth. Before you roll your eyes and think, *"Here we go, another marketing lecture,"* I promise you this isn't your typical spiel. This is about practical, actionable insights to advance your business.

The Importance of Modern Marketing

Let's start with the basics. Marketing isn't what it used to be. Gone are the days when you could rely solely on newspaper ads, word of mouth, or even a well-placed billboard. Today's marketing landscape is dynamic, digital, and constantly evolving. If you're not keeping up, you're falling behind.

Modern marketing isn't just about having a website or a Facebook page. It's about engaging with your audience where they are, providing value, and building relationships. It's about being seen as a thought leader in your industry, not just a seller of products or services.

Common Marketing Mistakes

I've seen many business owners make the same mistakes repeatedly. Let's talk about a few of these pitfalls:

1. **Sticking to Old Habits:** *"If it ain't broke, don't fix it"* is a dangerous mindset in

marketing. What worked five years ago might not work today. For instance, relying solely on traditional advertising while ignoring social media or email marketing can limit your reach significantly.

2. **Being Too Clever:** It's tempting to create a marketing campaign that's quirky or cute. But it's a wasted effort if your audience doesn't get the message. Clarity trumps cleverness every time.

3. **Ignoring Data:** In today's world, data is your best friend. Not analyzing your marketing campaigns means you're flying blind. You need to know what's working and what isn't so you can adjust your strategies accordingly.

4. **Lack of Consistency:** Marketing isn't a one-time effort. You must be consistent with your messaging, branding, and engagement. Sporadic efforts lead to sporadic results.

A Cautionary Tale

Let me share a story about John, a business owner I worked with a few years back. John owned a small chain of retail stores. He was proud of his traditional marketing methods: local word-of-mouth referrals, long-term sponsorships, and an occasional Val-Pak mailer. This worked well for him for years, but then sales declined.

John was resistant to change. He thought social media meant just having a page on Facebook and Instagram and that the one email per month he sent to clients was enough to keep them engaged with his brands. Despite my advice, he stuck to his guns. Unfortunately, his competitors didn't. They embraced digital marketing, engaged with customers online, and utilized data to refine their strategies.

The result? John's competitors saw significant growth while his business continued to struggle. Eventually, he had no choice but to close several stores. It was a tough lesson, but it highlighted the importance of modernizing marketing strategies.

The Power of Clear Messaging

I know it's easy to fall into the trap of trying to be witty or clever with your marketing campaigns. But here's the truth: clarity is key. Your customers need to understand what you're offering, why it matters, and how it benefits them.

Being clear doesn't mean being boring. It means being direct and ensuring your message resonates with your audience. When your message is clear, your customers don't have to guess what you're trying to say–they get it immediately, which drives action. It's important to remember that even if your product or service is obvious, such as buying a home or getting car insurance, the customer still has options and wants to work with businesses that best resonate with them.

Chapter Summary

Modern marketing is essential for business growth. Avoid common mistakes, focus on clarity, and embrace new strategies to stay ahead. Your business's future depends on it.

Action Items

1. **Audit Your Current Marketing Efforts:** Identify what's working and what isn't.
2. **Embrace Digital Marketing:** Invest time and resources in social media, email marketing, and SEO.
3. **Focus on Clear Messaging:** Ensure your marketing messages are direct and easy to understand.
4. **Use Data Analytics:** Track your campaigns and adjust based on performance data.
5. **Stay Consistent:** Develop a regular schedule for your marketing activities.
6. **Engage with Your Audience:** Build relationships with your customers through various channels.
7. **Stay Informed:** Keep up with the latest marketing trends and technologies.

BUSINESS
GBT+
BUSINESS
LGBTI+
BUSINES

8
Operations (modernize or die)

The line between disorder and order lies in logistics.
- Sun Tzu

Let's chat candidly about something that's probably been on your mind but may not get the attention it deserves: modernizing your operations. I know what you might be thinking: modernization sounds like a lot of work and expense. But here's the real kicker: failing to modernize isn't just a risky move; it's a business death sentence. Let's get into why embracing change is your ticket to growth.

The Trap of Complacency

First off, let's tackle a big issue–complacency. It's easy to get comfortable when things are going well. You've got a steady stream of customers, your revenue is solid, and your team seems content. But here's the problem: the business world is evolving at lightning speed. What worked yesterday might not work tomorrow. You risk falling behind when you become too satisfied with the status quo.

This is the part where I ask you if you remember Blockbuster. We all know the story. They ruled the video rental market until they didn't. Netflix came along with a modern approach, and the rest is history. Blockbuster's downfall wasn't due to one big mistake; it was a series of missed opportunities and a failure to adapt. The scary part is Blockbuster used to be a very singular story that was told to make the "dangers of complacency" point. Now, countless major companies and small businesses are falling victim to getting left behind.

In 2020, amid COVID, I launched a coaching program to help save as many businesses as possible. I was doing one-on-one calls all day to great personal satisfaction and mental exhaustion. I also began appearing frequently on my local CBS affiliate station to provide ideas and guidance to viewers hungry for information. One of the harsh realities during that time was that the people who had been putting off making operational changes were the ones who were punished the most by the market. For example, before COVID-19, I had politely suggested to the business owner of the hamburger place we would frequent that the fact he didn't offer online ordering dramatically reduced the amount of time we came to his business because his minimal staff made phone orders a nightmare. When COVID hit, he had no choice but to add it and was barely able to stay in business. The other thing that happened was he got whatever was out there and was the cheapest, so he solved one issue but created another: a poor online ordering experience.

The bottom line was that fewer people bought hamburgers from his business. We don't even think of that place anymore when we go out and get a burger. Our city has a Shake Shack now, and if you know, you know.

The Danger of Delayed Updates

Now, let's talk about updating your systems and processes. It's not uncommon for business owners to delay these updates because of the upfront costs or the perceived hassle. But think about it like this: every day you delay, you're losing potential efficiency gains. Modern tools and technologies can streamline operations, reduce errors, and save money in the long run. Delaying updates means you're effectively choosing to operate less efficiently than you could.

Common Mistakes to Avoid

1. **Ignoring Technology Trends:** It is crucial to stay updated with the latest technology

trends. Ignoring them can leave you miles behind your competition.

2. **Sticking to Outdated Processes:** Just because something has worked for years doesn't mean it's the best way to do it now. Regularly reviewing and updating your processes can reveal more efficient ways to get things done.

3. **Underestimating Customer Expectations:** Today's customers expect fast, seamless, and tech-savvy service. Falling behind in technology can lead to dissatisfied customers.

4. **Neglecting Employee Training:** Investing in new technology is pointless if your team doesn't know how to use it effectively. Continuous training is key.

5. **Overlooking Data Security:** Modernizing isn't just about efficiency but also security. Outdated systems are more vulnerable to cyberattacks.

Death by a Thousand Cuts

Business failure often doesn't happen overnight. It's typically the result of "death by a thousand cuts"—small issues that accumulate over time. Maybe it's a few too many manual processes that slow things down or outdated software that keeps crashing. Each minor issue might seem manageable on its own, but together they can cripple your business.

Chapter Summary

Modernizing your operations is essential for business growth. Complacency and delayed updates can lead to inefficiencies and eventual failure. Business decline is often gradual, resulting from numerous small issues rather than a single event.

Action Items

1. **Audit Your Current Systems:** Identify areas where outdated technology or processes hold you back.

2. **Stay Informed:** Keep up with industry trends and new technologies.
3. **Customer Feedback:** Regularly gather and act on customer feedback to ensure your offerings meet their expectations.
4. **Employee Training:** Invest in ongoing training for your team to ensure they can leverage new technologies effectively.
5. **Review Security Measures:** Ensure your systems are up to date with the latest security protocols.
6. **Invest in Automation:** Look for repetitive tasks that can be automated to save time and reduce errors.
7. **Set Regular Review Intervals:** Establish a schedule for regular reviews of your systems and processes to ensure they remain current.

SHP!

9
People (it takes a village)

The strength of the team is each individual member. The strength of each member is the team.
- Phil Jackson

No matter how many people refer to themselves as self-made, nobody does it all alone. Recruiting and retaining quality employees is one of the most persistent challenges businesses face today. As a business consultant and coach, I've seen firsthand how even the most promising companies can stumble when building a strong team. This chapter will explore why so many businesses struggle in this area, share some eye-opening statistics, and offer practical advice to rethink your people strategy.

Let's get started!

Why Businesses Struggle with Recruitment and Retention

Businesses often find themselves in a perpetual cycle of hiring and losing employees. The reasons for this are manifold, but they typically boil down to a few key issues:

1. **Lack of a Structured Hiring Process:** Many businesses lack a clear, consistent approach to hiring, which leads to hasty decisions and poor fits.

2. **Ineffective Onboarding:** The first few months are critical for new hires. New employees can feel lost without a structured onboarding process, leading to early turnover.

3. **Inadequate Engagement and Feedback:** Businesses often overlook the importance of regular feedback and engagement, resulting in employees feeling undervalued and disconnected.

The Importance of Employee Feedback and Engagement

Engaging employees and actively seeking their feedback can significantly impact retention and satisfaction.

Consider these statistics:

- **Gallup** found that companies with high employee engagement experience 21% higher profitability.

- **SHRM** reports that organizations with a structured employee feedback process see 14.9% lower turnover rates.

- **Officevibe** notes that 4 out of 10 workers are actively disengaged when they get little or no feedback.

Understanding Employee Engagement

Employee engagement can be categorized into three types:

1. **Engaged:** These employees are passionate, committed, and proactive. They are your top performers who drive innovation and productivity.

2. **Disengaged:** These employees do the bare minimum. They're not particularly invested in the company's success and are often just there for the paycheck.

3. **Actively Disengaged:** These employees are unhappy and may even undermine the company's efforts. They are detrimental to the workplace culture and productivity.

Rethinking Your People Strategy

Given these insights, it's clear why a solid people strategy is essential. Here are some reasons to rethink your approach:

1. **Improved Morale and Productivity:** Engaged employees are more productive and contribute to a positive work environment.

2. **Lower Turnover Rates:** A robust engagement and feedback system can help retain top talent.

3. **Better Cultural Fit:** A clear hiring process ensures that new hires align with your company's values and culture.

Vetting Processes for Freelancers, Gig Workers, and Contractors

In today's gig economy, freelancers and contractors play a crucial role. Here's why you should have a vetting process in place for them:

1. **Consistency and Quality:** Proper vetting ensures that freelancers and contractors deliver consistent, high-quality work.

2. **Cultural Fit:** Even temporary workers should align with your company's culture to maintain a cohesive work environment.

3. **Reliability:** A thorough vetting process helps you select reliable freelancers who can meet deadlines and contribute effectively.

Common Mistakes in Hiring and Firing

1. **Taking Too Long to Hire:** While it's important to find the right fit, taking too long can lead to losing top candidates to other offers.

2. **Delayed Terminations:** Holding onto employees who are no longer a good fit can harm your company's morale and productivity. It's essential to make timely decisions for the benefit of the team.

Chapter Summary

To transform your approach to recruiting, training, and retaining employees, consider the following steps:

Action Items

1. **Review and Revamp Your Hiring Process:** Ensure it's structured, consistent, and aligned with your company's values.
2. **Implement Regular Feedback Mechanisms:** Schedule regular check-ins and feedback sessions with all employees.
3. **Develop an Engaging Onboarding Process:** Make new hires feel welcome and supported from day one.
4. **Train Your Interviewers:** Ensure they are skilled in assessing both technical skills and cultural fit.
5. **Create a Vetting Process for Freelancers:** Treat them as an extension of your team.
6. **Monitor Employee Engagement Levels:** Use surveys and feedback tools to gauge and improve engagement.

7. **Act Quickly on Hiring and Firing Decisions:** Be decisive to maintain a high-performing team.

Part Three: The 5 Pillars In Action (or how to use them to grow your business)

GREAT
POSITIVE
MINDSET
POSITIVE
MINDSET
MINDSET

10
Positioned For Growth™ Mindset

The only limit to our realization of tomorrow will be our doubts of today.
- Franklin D. Roosevelt

A growth mindset is a crucial element in the Positioned For Growth™ framework. Let's explore three key concepts that will transform how you approach business growth: Becoming the Customer, Ending Who-Else-Itis, and Understanding the Power of Beliefs, Attitudes, and Actions.

Concept 1: Become the Customer

Understanding your customer is more than just knowing their demographics; it's about stepping into their shoes and experiencing your business from their perspective. This approach can drastically improve your decision-making process and business strategies.

How to Become the Customer:

1. **Customer Personas:** Create detailed profiles of your ideal customers. Include their preferences, challenges, and purchasing behaviors.

2. **Customer Journey Mapping:** Outline your customers' steps from awareness to purchase. Identify pain points and opportunities for improvement.

3. **Engage Directly:** Gather feedback through surveys, focus groups, and direct interactions. Understand their needs and expectations.

4. **Competitive Analysis:** Study your competitors' customers and see what draws them there. What can you learn and implement in your own business?

5. **Future-Proofing:** Regularly reassess your ideal customer. As markets evolve, ensure your target audience aligns with emerging trends and demands.

By becoming the customer, you not only enhance your products and services but also foster stronger customer loyalty and satisfaction.

Concept 2: End Who-Else-Itis

Who-Else-Itis is a condition where businesses rely on others' success with a product or service to validate their own decisions. This mindset can hinder innovation and delay strategic growth.

Understanding and Overcoming Who-Else-Itis:

1. **Medical Metaphor:** Just as bronchitis or bursitis is detrimental to health, Who-Else-Itis is harmful to business growth. It prevents you from being a pioneer and can make your business stagnant. This concept revolves around having you stop basing growth decisions when looking at a product or service on "who else" is doing it.

2. **First Mover Advantage:** The first company to adopt a new strategy or technology often gains significant competitive advantages, including brand recognition and customer loyalty.

3. **Embrace Boldness:** Identify and act on unique opportunities tailored to your business. Don't wait for others to validate your ideas. Evaluate risks, but don't shy away from being the first.

4. **Innovative Culture:** Foster a culture of innovation within your team. Encourage

creative thinking and reward bold initiatives.

5. **Strategic Implementation:** When considering new tools or strategies, focus on how they align with your specific goals rather than who else is using them.

By ending Who-Else-Itis, you position your business as a leader rather than a follower, giving you a competitive edge.

Concept 3: Belief Drives Attitude, Attitude Drives Actions, Actions Drive Results

Your beliefs shape your attitude, which in turn influences your actions and ultimately determines your results. This concept is fundamental for personal and business growth.

Applying This Principle:

1. **Beliefs:** Your core beliefs about your abilities and business potential set the stage.

Positive, growth-oriented beliefs foster resilience and innovation.

2. **Attitude:** A positive attitude stems from strong beliefs. It influences how you approach challenges and opportunities.

3. **Actions:** Attitudes drive proactive and strategic actions. Consistent, positive actions lead to desirable outcomes.

4. **Leadership:** As a leader, your belief-attitude-action framework influences your entire organization. A positive belief system encourages a motivated and productive team.

5. **Decision-Making:** Apply this framework in hiring, sales, marketing, and operations. Strong beliefs and attitudes lead to better decisions and superior results.

By nurturing positive beliefs, maintaining a proactive attitude, and executing strategic actions, you pave the way for remarkable business growth and success.

Chapter Summary

This chapter explored three critical concepts for fostering a growth mindset: becoming the customer, ending Who-Else-Itis, and understanding the power of beliefs, attitudes, and actions. These principles will guide you to make informed, innovative, and bold decisions, driving your business toward unprecedented growth.

Action Items

1. **Create Customer Personas:** Develop detailed profiles of your ideal customers.
2. **Map Customer Journeys:** Identify and improve touchpoints in the customer experience.
3. **Engage with Customers:** Gather direct feedback through surveys and focus groups.
4. **Conduct Competitive Analysis:** Learn from competitors and future-proof your customer base.
5. **Identify Unique Opportunities:** Focus on strategies tailored to your business, not others.

6. **Foster Innovation:** Encourage and reward creative thinking within your team.
7. **Implement the Belief-Attitude-Action Framework:** Apply this principle to all business aspects.

NEW
RECORD
NEW
SALES
RECORD
NEW
SALES RECORD

11
Positioned For Growth™ Sales

Earlier, we highlighted the critical role a modern sales strategy plays in business growth. Now, let's look at three essential concepts that can transform your sales strategy and position you for substantial growth. I want to introduce you to the "Assess Your Value First" strategy, explain the importance of "Challenging Your Sales Versatility," and share why "Best Practices Kill Sales Growth."

Concept 1: Assess Your Value First Strategy

Let's start with the "Assess Your Value First" strategy. This concept is all about leading with value in every customer interaction. In the context of selling, this means your primary focus should be on understanding and delivering the unique value that your product or service offers to your customers.

What is a Value First Strategy?

A value-first strategy prioritizes the customer's needs and problems over the sales pitch. Instead of diving straight into the features and benefits of your product, you begin by identifying what the customer truly needs and how you can help them achieve their goals or solve their problems. This approach builds trust and positions you as a valuable partner rather than just another vendor.

Implementing a Value-First Strategy:

1. **Research and Understand:** Before any interaction, research your prospect's

industry, company, and specific challenges they face.

2. **Ask the Right Questions:** During initial conversations, ask insightful questions that uncover their pain points and objectives.

3. **Tailor Your Pitch:** Once you understand their needs, tailor your pitch to highlight how your solution specifically addresses their problems and adds value.

Adopting a value-first strategy creates a strong foundation of trust and relevance, making prospects more likely to be receptive to your sales pitch and ultimately become loyal customers.

Concept 2: Challenge Your Sales Versatility

Next, let's discuss the importance of challenging your sales versatility. Today's buyers are diverse in how they prefer to communicate and engage with sales professionals. Limiting yourself to one or two methods of communication can hinder your ability to connect with potential customers.

Diversify Your Engagement Methods:

1. **Phone Calls:** Still effective, especially for building personal connections and handling complex discussions.

2. **Emails:** Ideal for detailed information, follow-ups, and formal communications.

3. **Chat:** Great for quick, real-time responses and addressing immediate queries.

4. **Video Calls:** Provide a more personal touch and can be crucial for product demonstrations and face-to-face interactions.

5. **Text Messages:** Perfect for brief updates, reminders, and check-ins.

Why Diversify?

Diversifying your engagement methods allows you to meet prospects where they are most comfortable. Some prefer the personal touch of a phone call, while others might favor the convenience of a text message. Being versatile increases your chances of reaching and resonating with a broader audience.

How to Implement Versatility:

1. **Know Your Audience:** Understand the preferred communication methods of your target market.

2. **Be Adaptable:** Be prepared to switch between different modes of communication based on the prospect's preferences.

3. **Invest in Tools:** Utilize CRM systems and communication platforms that allow seamless integration of various communication channels.

Challenging your sales versatility ensures you are always in tune with your prospects' preferences, thereby enhancing your ability to connect and close deals.

Concept 3: Realize That Best Practices Kill Sales Growth

Lastly, let's address a counterintuitive concept: that best practices can kill sales growth. While best practices are often touted as the gold standard, relying solely on them can limit your potential.

Why Best Practices Can Be Limiting

Best practices are, by definition, methods and techniques that are widely accepted and used because they are effective. However, they are also average ideas everyone uses, which means they don't provide a competitive edge. You must go beyond these established norms to excel and truly grow your sales.

Front of the Learning Curve Ideas

Instead of sticking to best practices, focus on innovative, cutting-edge strategies that put you ahead of the curve. This involves continuous learning, experimenting with new approaches, and staying ahead of industry trends.

Implementing Innovative Strategies:

1. **Continuous Learning:** Invest in ongoing education and training for yourself and your team.

2. **Experimentation:** Encourage a culture of experimentation where new ideas are tested and refined.

3. **Stay Informed:** Keep up with the latest industry trends, technologies, and methodologies.

Moving beyond best practices and embracing innovation, you can create unique strategies that set you apart from the competition and drive exceptional sales growth.

Chapter Summary

This chapter discussed the importance of leading with value, diversifying your sales engagement methods, and going beyond best practices to achieve exceptional sales growth. Implementing these concepts will position you for success in today's competitive market.

Action Items

1. **Conduct** thorough research on your prospects before every interaction.
2. **Develop** a list of insightful questions to uncover customer needs.
3. **Tailor** your sales pitch to focus on the value you provide.
4. **Diversify** your communication methods to include phone, email, chat, video, and text.
5. **Identify** the preferred communication channels of your target audience.
6. **Foster** a culture of continuous learning and experimentation within your team.
7. **Stay** informed about industry trends and new sales techniques.

SUCCESS
SUCCCESS
SUCCESS
MARKETING PLAN
SUCCESSS
MARKETING PLAN
MARKETING PLAN

12
Positioned For Growth™ Marketing

Marketing takes a day to learn. Unfortunately, it takes a lifetime to master.
- Philip Kotler

Welcome to the world of modern marketing, where the landscape constantly evolves, and staying ahead requires more than just traditional strategies. As a business owner, you're likely bombarded with countless tips and tricks promising to skyrocket your growth. I get all the ads online like you do, but let's cut through the noise and focus on what truly matters. In this chapter, we're diving into three pivotal concepts forming part of the Positioned

For Growth™ framework. These concepts are designed to help you refine your marketing approach, ensuring you attract and retain more customers.

Let's get started.

Concept 1: Focus on Tangible Versus Intangible "Why Buy" Strategies

Let's start with a crucial insight: when it comes to marketing, what you highlight about your product or service must be tangible. Consumers want to know what they're getting and why it's valuable to them. Talking about how long you've been in business or how many awards you've won might be impressive, but these intangible points don't necessarily translate into more customers.

Take, for instance, a car dealership. Advertising that you have the largest selection of cars in the area is an intangible benefit; it's not something a customer can directly experience or measure. On the other hand, offering free lifetime inspections as long as the customer owns their vehicle is a tangible benefit. It's clear, measurable, and directly valuable to the customer. This kind of tangible offer can significantly impact a buyer's decision-making process.

In your marketing efforts, ask yourself: *"What concrete benefits am I offering that will directly improve my customer's life or solve their problems?"* These tangible benefits are what will attract and retain customers.

Concept 2: Stop Ignoring Marketing Channels You Don't Understand

It's easy to stick with what you know, but the marketing landscape is constantly evolving. Just because you're unfamiliar with a new platform or strategy doesn't mean you should ignore it. In fact, saying yes to new opportunities can open significant growth for your business.

Take TikTok, for example. It might have started as a platform for teens, but its user demographics have shifted dramatically. In recent years, many TikTok users have become adults with purchasing power. Did you know that the average TikTok user is no longer just a teenager? My 78-year-old mother, for instance, is a frequent shopper on TikTok, much to my amazement (and occasional frustration).

This shift demonstrates the importance of exploring new channels. You don't need to be an expert in every new platform to succeed. Instead, invest in smart people–whether they are part of your internal team or external partners–who can navigate these channels effectively. This approach ensures you don't leave potential revenue on the table due to a lack of understanding or familiarity.

Concept 3: Remember That Clarity Always Wins

In the age of information overload, simplicity and clarity are your best friends. Consumers are bombarded with messages every day, and the ones that stand out are those that are clear and direct.

Gone are the days when overly clever or complex marketing messages were the norm. Today's successful companies focus on how they can solve problems for their customers and demonstrate their expertise through clear, concise messaging. This shift towards clarity and thought leadership builds trust and shows competence.

I encourage you to take a hard look at your current marketing and brand messaging. Are your taglines, website, and overall value proposition clear? Do they quickly communicate what you offer and why it matters to the customer? Challenge yourself to update and simplify your messages to ensure they resonate immediately with your audience.

Chapter Summary

In summary, modern marketing focuses on tangible benefits, explores new channels, and maintains clear messaging. These strategies are essential to driving growth and staying ahead of the competition.

Action Items

1. **Audit Your Marketing Messages:** Identify and highlight tangible benefits in your marketing materials.
2. **Explore New Channels:** Research and test at least one new marketing platform you are currently not using.
3. **Hire Smart Marketers:** Invest in talented marketing professionals who understand the latest trends and platforms.
4. **Simplify Your Messaging:** Ensure all your marketing messages are clear, concise, and customer focused.
5. **Update Your Website:** Revamp your website to reflect your clear value proposition and solve customers' problems.
6. **Monitor Demographics:** Regularly review the demographics of your marketing

channels to ensure they align with your target audience.

7. **Engage Consistently:** Develop a consistent marketing schedule and stick to it to maintain a strong presence.

13
Positioned For Growth™ Operations

In the end, all business operations can be reduced to three words: people, product, and profits.
- Lee Iacocca

As a business owner, you've likely heard the saying, *"Operations are the backbone of a successful business."* It's true—efficient operations can mean the difference between a thriving enterprise and one that merely survives. But what does it really take to optimize your operations for growth? In this chapter, we'll delve into three critical concepts that form part of the Positioned For Growth™ framework. These concepts aren't just theoretical–they are practical, actionable strategies designed to help you enhance productivity, ensure customer-centricity, and invest in continuous development. Let's explore how you can implement these strategies to drive your business toward sustained success.

Concept 1: Don't Mandate Productivity

Imagine trying to command a garden to grow faster just by yelling at the plants. It sounds ridiculous, right? Yet, many business owners attempt a similar approach by simply mandating productivity. You can't just tell your team to work harder or demand more from your suppliers and vendors. This top-down directive approach rarely leads to sustainable improvements and can even create resentment and burnout.

Instead, focus on a strategy that explains, engages, and supports your team. Here are a few ways to implement this:

1. **Explain the "Why":** When introducing new goals or changes, always communicate the reasons behind them. People are more likely to be motivated if they understand the bigger picture and how their efforts contribute to the company's success.

2. **Engage Your Team:** Involve your employees in problem-solving and decision-making processes. This not only makes them feel valued but also leverages their unique insights and experiences, often leading to more innovative solutions.

3. **Support with Resources:** Ensure your team has the necessary tools, training, and support to meet the expectations set for them. This might include new technology, additional staffing, or professional development opportunities.

By shifting from a mandate-driven approach to one that fosters collaboration and empowerment, you'll create an environment where productivity can naturally thrive.

Concept 2: Is Your Policy Customer-Centric or Business-Centric?

Take a moment to review your current operational policies and procedures. Are they designed for the convenience of your business or the satisfaction of your customers? This distinction is crucial because customer-centric policies often lead to higher average transactions and better long-term customer retention.

Consider a policy as simple as return and exchange processes. A business-centric policy might impose strict deadlines and cumbersome requirements for returns to minimize the business's hassle. Conversely, a customer-centric policy is flexible, hassle-free, and designed to enhance customer experience, even if it means more work for the business.

A local bookstore's rigid return policy frustrated many loyal customers. After receiving feedback, the owner adopted a more lenient, customer-friendly approach. This change increased customer satisfaction, more frequent purchases, and a noticeable boost in word-of-mouth referrals.

When evaluating your policies, ask yourself: *"Is this making things easier for my business or my customers?"* Prioritizing customer-centric policies will foster loyalty and encourage repeat business.

Concept 3: Maintaining Active Investment in Team and Customer Experience Development

No matter the size of your company, continuous investment in your team's development and customer experience is non-negotiable if you aim for growth. This commitment should be a permanent part of your budget and ingrained in your company's culture.

1. **Team Development:** Regular training programs are essential. Whether upskilling your team on the latest industry trends or providing leadership training for potential

managers, continuous learning keeps your team agile and motivated.

2. **Customer Experience Enhancement:** Invest in technology and services that improve the customer experience. This might include CRM systems, improved customer service channels, or user-friendly e-commerce platforms.

3. However, be wary of fads. Invest in technologies and services with a proven track record and robust infrastructure. Your goal is to enhance efficiency and customer satisfaction, not to jump on the latest bandwagon.

Create a detailed training and development plan within your organization. Regularly review the age and effectiveness of your current systems and stay informed about advancements that might better suit your evolving needs.

Chapter Summary

In this chapter, we discussed three essential concepts for operational excellence: avoiding productivity mandates, prioritizing customer-centric policies, and investing in continuous team and customer experience development. These strategies form the backbone of sustainable growth in the Positioned For Growth™ framework.

Action Items

1. **Communicate** the reasons behind new goals and changes to your team.
2. **Involve** employees in problem-solving and decision-making.
3. **Provide** the necessary tools and resources for your team to succeed.
4. **Review** operational policies to ensure they prioritize customer convenience.
5. **Implement** regular training and development programs for your team.
6. **Invest** in technology that enhances customer experience.

7. **Conduct** periodic reviews of systems and processes to ensure they remain effective and up-to-date.

14
Positioned For Growth™ People

Coming together is a beginning; keeping together is progress; working together is success.
- Henry Ford

It's time to optimize the most crucial element of your business–your people. Whether they are full-time employees, freelancers, gig workers, or contractors, effectively leveraging your team can drive significant growth. In this chapter, we'll explore three essential concepts that will help you harness the power of your workforce: avoiding rescue hires, mastering the art of interviewing, and implementing a 90-day stay plan for new hires.

Concept 1: Stop Making Rescue Hires

Let's start with a common pitfall many business owners fall into–making rescue hires. A rescue hire is when you urgently fill a position out of desperation, without proper vetting or consideration of the long-term fit. This usually happens when there's a sudden vacancy or an immediate need for skills. You might feel under pressure to plug the gap quickly, but this often leads to hiring the wrong person.

Rescue hires can be detrimental to your business. They can drain resources, reduce team morale, and ultimately harm your company's performance. It's crucial to maintain a clear head when recruiting. Even under pressure, take the time to thoroughly evaluate candidates. Focus on finding the right fit rather than just a warm body to fill the seat.

Encouragement: It's better to wait for the right candidate than to rush and make a mistake that could cost you more in the long run. Stick to your hiring principles and trust the process. You'll thank yourself later when you have a competent, cohesive team driving your business forward.

Concept 2: Understand That Interviewing is a Skill

Just because you're a business owner, executive, or manager doesn't mean you're inherently equipped to interview and vet candidates effectively. Interviewing is a skill, and like any skill, it requires practice and continuous learning. Modern interviewing techniques and strategies have evolved, and staying up-to-date is essential.

Investing in learning how to interview properly can significantly impact the quality of your hires. This applies to everyone you bring into your business, whether they're employees, contractors, freelancers, or gig workers.

Effective interviewing helps you identify not just the skills and experience of a candidate, but also their cultural fit and potential to grow within your company.

Consider training sessions or workshops on interviewing techniques. Role-playing scenarios and feedback sessions can be incredibly beneficial. Remember, the goal is to create a structured and consistent interview process that allows you to compare candidates fairly and make informed decisions.

Concept 3: Create and Implement a 90-Day Stay Plan for New Hires

Instead of focusing on fear-based 90-day probation periods, shift your mindset to creating a supportive environment for new hires. A well-thought-out 90-day stay plan can significantly improve employee retention and satisfaction.

An effective 90-day stay plan should include:

- A welcome lunch with the owner or key executives to build rapport.
- Regular check-ins to ensure the new hire feels supported and heard.
- Active solicitation of feedback to understand their experience and address any concerns.
- Structured training sessions to equip them with the necessary tools and knowledge.
- Assigning a mentor or buddy to guide them through the initial days.
- Clear communication of expectations and goals for the first 90 days.
- Opportunities for social integration within the team include team-building activities or informal gatherings.

Research supports that employers actively engaging with their new hires can reduce turnover and significantly increase retention rates. For example, a Society for Human Resource Management (SHRM) study found that companies with a structured onboarding process experience 50% greater new hire productivity and 82% better retention rates.

Chapter Summary

In summary, to leverage your team for growth, avoid rescue hires, develop your interviewing skills, and implement a supportive 90-day stay plan for new hires. These strategies will help you build a stronger, more cohesive workforce that can drive your business to new heights.

Action Items

1. **Assess** your current hiring process and identify areas prone to rescue hires.
2. **Develop** a clear, consistent interview process and invest in training for key team members.
3. **Design** a comprehensive 90-day stay plan for all new hires.
4. **Schedule** regular check-ins and feedback sessions with new hires.
5. **Assign** mentors or buddies to new employees to help them integrate smoothly.
6. **Organize** welcome events and team-building activities to foster a positive work culture.

7. **Monitor and evaluate** the effectiveness of your onboarding process and make adjustments as needed.

Cory Mosley

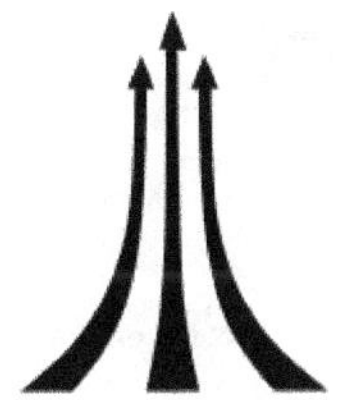

Part Four:
Get Going, Get Growing

15
The 3 W's (or how to change any process in your business fast)

Without continual growth and progress, such words as improvement, achievement, and success have no meaning.
- Benjamin Franklin

We already know that the word change can send shivers down the spine of even the most seasoned business owner. But what if I told you there's a straightforward method to change and improve any process within your business effectively?

Enter the Three W's: What, Why, and What Better. These three simple questions can be your guiding light, helping you dissect and enhance your business operations precisely and clearly.

The Three W's Process

Let's break it down. The Three W's method involves asking three critical questions about any process in your business:

1. **What are we doing now?**
2. **Why are we doing it that way?**
3. **What better process can we find to improve?**

What Are We Doing Now?

The first step is to understand the current process. It's essential to map out exactly what you're doing now. This means documenting each step, understanding the workflow, and identifying the resources involved. By doing this, you get a clear picture of the existing process, which is crucial for any improvement initiative.

Example: Imagine you run a small manufacturing business, and you're looking at your inventory management process. The first question you ask is, *"What are we doing now?"* You discover that your team manually counts inventory at the end of each day and updates the stock levels in a spreadsheet. This manual process is time-consuming and prone to errors.

Why Are We Doing It That Way?

Next, delve into the rationale behind the current process. Understanding the "why" helps uncover the reasons, habits, or constraints that led to the existing method. This step often reveals outdated practices or assumptions that no longer serve your business well.

Example: When you ask, *"Why are we doing it that way?"* you find out that manual counting started years ago when your business was much smaller and you didn't have the budget for sophisticated software. However, your business has grown significantly, and what worked then isn't efficient now.

What Better Process Can We Find to Improve?

Finally, brainstorm and research better alternatives. This is where innovation and creativity come into play. Look for new technologies, methods, or strategies to streamline operations and improve efficiency.

Example: You explore various inventory management software options for your inventory management. You choose a system that integrates with your sales platform, automatically updates stock levels in real time, and provides detailed analytics. This change reduces manual errors, saves time, and provides valuable insights to manage your inventory better.

Applying the Three W's: Another Example

Let's consider another scenario. You own a customer service agency and have received feedback that response times are slow.

1. **What are we doing now?** You find that customer inquiries are managed through a shared email inbox, with agents manually assigning and responding to tickets.

2. **Why are we doing it that way?** This method was set up when the agency first started, as it was cost-effective and simple. However, the volume of inquiries has since grown.

3. **What better process can we find to improve?** You research and implement a customer service platform that automatically categorizes and prioritizes tickets, assigns them to available agents based on their expertise, and tracks response times. This upgrade enhances efficiency, reduces response times, and improves customer satisfaction.

Chapter Summary

This chapter introduced the Three W's method: What are we doing now? Why are we doing it that way? What better process can we find to improve? By asking these questions, business owners can systematically identify and enhance inefficient processes, leading to increased productivity and better outcomes.

Action Items

1. **Document Current Processes:** Map out your current workflows in detail.
2. **Identify Rationale:** Understand why each process is in place.
3. **Evaluate Alternatives:** Research new tools, technologies, and methods.
4. **Pilot New Processes:** Test new processes on a small scale before full implementation.
5. **Train Your Team:** Ensure your team is well-trained in any new processes or technologies.
6. **Monitor Performance:** Regularly review the performance of new processes and make adjustments as needed.

7. **Seek Feedback:** Gather feedback from your team and customers to continually improve.

BUSINESS
D.I.Y
DO IT
GROWTH
BUSINESS

16
The Positioned For Growth™ D.I.Y. Plan

Vision without action is a daydream.
Action without vision is a nightmare.
- Japanese Proverb

GET POSITIONED FOR GROWTH™

Step1	Step2	Step 3
Conduct Your Own 5 Pillars Assessment	Ask The 3 W Questions	Take Relentless Action

Visit CoryMosley.com/assessment to access free assessment resources.

MOMENTUM
KEEP
MOMENTUM
TO KEP
MOMENTUM
GOING
TO KEEPEP MOMENTUM
GOING

17
C.A.P.I. (or a formula to keep growth momentum)

Life is like riding a bicycle. To keep your balance, you must keep moving.
- Albert Einstein

In the fast-paced business world, growth is not just an aspiration–it's a necessity. For business owners, franchisees, and corporate CEOs alike, maintaining growth momentum is the lifeblood of continued success. Now, I want to introduce you to a powerful strategy that has proven to be a game-changer for many: the C.A.P.I. Method. C.A.P.I. stands for Celebrate, Assess, Plan, Implement, and it is a simple yet effective formula that can help you and your team achieve and sustain growth momentum.

Celebrate: Recognizing Wins Big and Small

The first step in the C.A.P.I. method is to Celebrate. Celebrating large and small achievements is essential for building a positive and motivated team culture. It acknowledges your team's hard work and dedication and reinforces the behaviors that lead to success. Celebrations can take many forms–public recognition in a team meeting, a congratulatory email, or even a small reward.

Daily Practice Options:

- Start each day with a brief team huddle where you highlight a recent achievement. This could be closing a sale, launching a new product, or even completing a challenging task.
- Encourage team members to share their personal wins and recognize their peers.

Weekly Practice Options:

- Hold a "Win of the Week" session where the team gathers to celebrate the most significant achievements of the week.
- Create a "Wall of Fame" in your office or a virtual equivalent where you display and update these wins regularly.

By celebrating consistently, you build a culture of appreciation and motivation, which lays the foundation for continuous growth.

Assess: Understanding the Current State

After celebrating successes, the next step is to Assess. This involves critically examining your current situation and identifying what is working well and what isn't. Honest and thorough assessments help you understand your strengths, weaknesses, opportunities, and threats.

Daily Practice Options:

- Set aside a few minutes at the end of each day to review what went well and what could have been better. Encourage team members to do the same and share their insights.
- Use quick surveys or feedback tools to gather immediate input from your team.

Weekly Practice Options:

- Conduct a more in-depth analysis at the end of each week. Review key performance indicators (KPIs) and metrics to understand trends and patterns.
- Hold a team meeting to discuss these findings openly, fostering a culture of transparency and continuous improvement.

Assessment ensures you are always aware of your business's current state, enabling informed decision-making.

Plan: Charting the Path Forward

With a clear understanding of your current situation, the next step is to Plan. Planning involves setting specific, measurable, achievable, relevant, and time-bound (SMART) goals and developing strategies and action plans to achieve these goals.

Daily Practice Options:

- Dedicate a few minutes each day to review your daily goals and priorities. Adjust them based on your assessments and any new information.
- Encourage your team to set and share daily goals, fostering accountability and focus.

Weekly Practice Options:

- At the start of each week, hold a planning session where you set the week's goals and outline the key actions required to achieve them.
- Ensure that each team member understands their role and

responsibilities for the week and how their work aligns with the overall objectives.

Effective planning keeps your team focused and aligned, ensuring everyone works towards the same goals.

Implement: Taking Action and Executing Plans

The final step in the C.A.P.I. method is Implement. This is where the rubber meets the road. Implementation is all about executing your plans efficiently and effectively. It requires discipline, commitment, and the ability to adapt as needed.

Daily Practice:

- Start each day with a clear action plan. Break down your tasks into manageable chunks and tackle them one at a time.
- Encourage your team to do the same and provide support and resources as needed.

Weekly Practice:

- Review progress at the end of each week. Celebrate successes, assess challenges or obstacles, and adjust plans as necessary.
- Foster a culture of accountability by having team members report on their progress and share any lessons learned.

Consistent and disciplined implementation turns plans into reality and drives continuous growth.

Putting It All Together

The C.A.P.I. method–Celebrate, Assess, Plan, Implement–is a powerful formula for maintaining growth momentum in your business. Making these practices a regular part of your daily and weekly routines creates a dynamic and responsive organization that is always moving forward.

- **Celebrate** achievements to build a motivated and positive team culture.

- **Assess** your current situation to make informed decisions.
- **Plan** your actions to stay focused and aligned with your goals.
- **Implement** your plans with discipline and commitment to achieve tangible results.

By integrating the C.A.P.I. method into your business practices, you empower yourself and your team to achieve sustained growth and success. Make this method a habit, and watch as your business thrives, adapts, and grows in an ever-changing world.

Epilogue
The future of business vs. your future in business

As we reach the conclusion of *Positioned For Growth™: A Proven Framework to Modernize Your Business and Achieve Record Revenues*, I want to leave you with a vision for your future.

In a world where politics, the economy, and global issues seem to shift like the sands in a desert, it's crucial to stay laser-focused on what you can control: your business.

As business owners, you are the backbone of the economy, the lifeblood of innovation, and the torchbearers of the entrepreneurial spirit. The world may be unpredictable, but your determination, creativity, and willingness to take calculated risks can shape a future filled with unprecedented opportunities and record profits.

Remember, the Positioned For Growth™ framework isn't just a set of guidelines; it's a mindset. It's about staying ahead of the game, continuously adapting, and finding new ways to capture and keep a competitive edge in your marketplace. This framework is your toolkit for navigating the challenges and seizing the opportunities that come your way.

The future of business is in constant flux, driven by technological advancements, changing consumer behaviors, and global trends. But you have the power to shape your future in business. You can survive and thrive in any environment by staying relentless in your focus, committed to innovation, and dedicated to excellence.

Think of yourself as a creator and an innovator. You have the power to turn ideas into reality, bring new products and services to market, and solve problems in ways no one else can. Your willingness to embrace change, to take risks, and to push boundaries is what sets you apart. It will keep you ahead of the competition and enable you to achieve record revenues.

I believe in your potential to accomplish more than you ever thought possible. The path of entrepreneurship or executive leadership is not easy, but it is immensely rewarding. You are the stewards of economic growth, the champions of innovation, and the architects of a brighter future. Your journey doesn't end here; it is just beginning.

Stay focused, stay inspired, and keep pushing forward. Use the Positioned For Growth™ framework as your guide, and let your vision, passion, and determination lead the way. The future of business is bright, and your future in business is limitless. Together, we can build a world where entrepreneurs and leaders like you continue to drive progress, create jobs, and shape the future.

Thank you for embarking on this journey with me. Know that I am here to help and support you along the way. Whether that is directly working with your company, presenting to organizations you are associated with, becoming your personal coach, or simply educating you via our podcast or videos, my mission remains the same: to help businesses modernize, grow, and achieve record revenues.

Here's to your continued growth and success.

- Cory

Acknowledgments

The creation of this book and my ability to help people and businesses across the country for the last twenty years is a result of a rock-solid support system that encourages me, provides me a space for humor, gives me grace, and doesn't judge. I'd like to thank a few of those people now.

My wife, Xiomara
Mom
The Mosley Family
Brandon G.
William H.
Dawne B.G.
Jamal & Liz
SVB & KB
Carlos & Simone
Mike & Mary
Delatorro

Cory Mosley

About The Author

Cory Mosley, CSP, is an award-winning business growth speaker, consultant, coach, and media personality known for successfully identifying and maximizing growth opportunities for businesses, associations, and corporations.

Cory's unique approach to business growth, which focuses on increasing sales, creating raving fans, and improving cash flow through the adoption of innovative ideas and strategies, has made him a sought-after consultant and speaker.

Accredited as a Certified Speaking Professional (CSP) by the National Speakers Association, Cory speaks frequently on business growth topics in sales, marketing, human capital, operations, and mindset.

With a diverse client list that includes family-owned small businesses and major corporations like Audi, Mercedes-Benz, Berkshire Hathaway, BBDO, and

General Motors, Cory has proven his ability to deliver results across a wide range of business contexts.

Cory is the author of three books, the founder of Mosley Strategy Group, the creator of streaming network RVASBN.com, and part of the ownership team of Pecan Jacks™ Ice Cream & Candy Kitchen, one of the fastest-growing sweet franchise brands in the country.

Cory has completed and achieved certifications from The Wharton School of Executive Education and High Point University.

Cory's professional achievements are complemented by his commitment to a balanced lifestyle. He resides in Henrico Country, Virginia, with his wife of 12 years, Xiomara, and two beloved dogs, Rozy Bear and Harlee, reflecting his dedication to family and personal well-being.

For more information about our speaking, consulting, coaching, and training products and services, please visit CORYMOSLEY.COM.

bitly
Scan me

Cory Mosley

www.ingramcontent.com/pod-product-compliance
Lightning Source LLC
Chambersburg PA
CBHW052131270326
41930CB00012B/2840
9798218465711